Dream your plan, plan your dream
7 STEPS TO MANIFESTING SUCCESS

TAMARA MITCHELL-DAVIS

CEO WIFE PUBLISHING

Copyright © 2022 by Tamara Mitchell-Davis

All rights reserved.

No part of this book may be reproduced in any form or by any electronic or mechanical means, including information storage and retrieval systems, without written permission from the author, except for the use of brief quotations in a book review.

This book reflects the author's present recollections of experiences over time. Some names and characteristics have been changed and some events have been compressed to protect one's identity and privacy.

Unless otherwise indicated, Bible quotations are from the Holy Bible, King James Version. All rights reserved.

Library of Congress Control Number: 2022908645

ISBN for paperback: 978-1-7375400-2-1
ISBN for eBook: 978-1-7375400-3-8
Published by CEO Wife Publishing
www.theceowife.com

This book is dedicated to the women who put everyone and everything else before themselves. My prayer is that you be enlightened, inspired and motivated to see all your hopes, goals and dreams become reality.

Contents

Foreword — vii

Introduction — 1
Step One — 6
Step Two — 12
Step Three — 20
Step Four — 27
Step Five — 34
Step Six — 43
Step Seven — 56
Afterword — 61

Acknowledgments — 75
About the Author — 77

Foreword

BY ENISHA LIGON-GARRETT

Growing up, I watched all the Disney movies. They showed us that all our dreams could come true if we just wished on a star. I expected to be whisked away into a magical world of beautiful dresses, singing animals, and happy endings with a handsome prince. While wishing on a star may not make our dreams come true, it starts there. It starts with the audacity to dream, not just dream, but dream big.

For far too many, this is where it stops in a perpetual cycle of tiny wishes that you never make come true so that you can have all that you dreamed.

But here is where I want to challenge you. Dreams and wishes are not the same. What's the difference between a wish and a dream? A wish is something we hope for. It's something we want, but we don't necessarily believe it will come true. A dream, on the other hand, is something we're passionate about and truly believe in. We wish all day. We wish that we had more money, we wish we could take an extra vacation day, we even wish we could eat an extra serving of pound cake without packing on unwanted calories. We dream of the day that we will be financially free; we dream of meeting the love of our lives; we dream of living a life filled with abundance and joy. Martin Luther King did not have a wish; he had a dream. When you have a dream, you have an unshakeable belief that you will achieve it. And with the right plan, you can. So what's your dream? What are you passionate about? What do you truly believe in? If you can answer those questions, then you have taken a critical first step.

The harsh reality is, as adults, we suppress our true desires because of fear. There's nothing more heartbreaking than watching someone give up on their dreams because of fear. Fear of failure, fear of the unknown, fear of not being good enough, and even the fear of success. These fears can create a powerful force that pulls us away from our dreams and prevents us from achieving our full potential. But, I want to tell you something: it's never too late to shift your focus and start chasing those dreams again. Just because you've fallen short before doesn't mean that your dreams won't come true. So get back up, fix your crown, and keep moving forward.

I can tell you this with such confidence because I have always been a big dreamer. And for a long time in my life, all of my dreams seemed to come true effortlessly. I never connected that I was naturally gifted at many things that I tried and was a hard worker with my successes. Talent and a little hard work are a winning combination; so many things just worked out for me. I thought it would be like that forever. However, as I got older, I began to dream bigger, and it became my responsibility solely to make my dreams come true. I quickly realized just how small I was playing. I was only chasing dreams that I knew would come true. I was not challenging myself or stepping outside my comfort zone. And when I decided to push more, I was confronted with failures. Yes, that is plural. Nothing seemed to work anymore.

We all know that you can only go so long without a win. We can only watch our dreams get further and further out of reach without feeling discontent. If we are not careful, depression can even set in. That is precisely what happened to me. After having my youngest daughter in 2010, I slipped into a deep depression. Some of it can be attributed to post-partum, but a lot was due to feeling like my dreams were no longer coming true. I had a good job, a loving family, and was in good physical health; that's the dream, right. Not for me; I always wanted more. I wanted Oprah+. I wanted to be an influential entrepreneur and have a thriving and loving family. But at this point in my life, I had neither. I'll be 100% transparent with you; there was a time when so much disappointment in myself had set in that I was unwilling to try. I took myself out of the game. I was not sitting on the bench, and I was in the locker room, ready to turn in my jersey. Something needed to change.

In 2016, we decided to move to California to be closer to my family, and I came across some of my old marketing materials, and they reminded me of just how dope I am. I had run a successful gorilla marketing company, generated hundreds of thousands of dollars in advertising revenue, and published several magazines for myself and my clients. This simple find connected me to when I felt like I was running towards my Oprah+ dreams. It is funny because my husband tried to get me to toss all of this memorabilia, and I knew it would serve a purpose one day. It was just what I needed to dream again. I have not stopped dreaming since that day.

This new excitement, coupled with a framework for accomplishing my goals, has led me to where I am today. I have a thriving branding agency, and I am the publisher of BWMB Magazine, a publication for Black Female Entrepreneurs.

If you are here reading this book, it's only for two reasons, you either have big dreams and don't know where to start to accomplish them, or you have not even allowed yourself to dream and are ready to dream.

I cannot imagine someone more qualified to guide you through this process. The process of becoming the kind of person who not only has the audacity to dream big but the kind of person who turns those dreams into goals and creates a plan to accomplish them so they can set bigger ones. Tamara has shown us time and time again what this process looks like in her life. You don't become a 7-time best-selling author and host sold-out events without a clear plan. She has also shown hundreds of women in her community how to go after their dreams. She is the recipient of countless awards such as: 100 Women of Color, I am HER International Woman on the Rise and Entrepreneur of the Year, and ACHI Magazine Award Orator of the Year, to name a few. Tamara continues to show us what living on purpose looks like. She has accumulated this long list of accolades because of the framework she shares with you in this book.

So, if you are looking for a roadmap to realizing your dreams or simply the inspiration to allow yourself to dream in the first place, then this book is for you. I am living proof that it is never too late to become who you were always meant to be. Keep dreaming and start planning!

Enisha Ligon-Garrett, Brand Strategist

CEO, Ellese & Co Creative
Founder of BWMB Magazine
Email: designteam@elleseandco.com
Website: www.elleseandco.com | www.bwmbmagazine.com
Facebook, Instagram and TikTok: @bwmbmagazine

Introduction

> "There is no limit to what we, as women, can accomplish."
>
> —Michelle Obama, #ForeverFLOTUS

Sometimes, we get in our own way. We don't believe in ourselves. We struggle with imposter syndrome. We don't follow through with the actions required to reach our goals, and we become easily discouraged. If you have found this book, it is likely that you want something to change; you want to develop your confidence; you want to prove to yourself you can succeed.

Perhaps you've lost sight of your goals. Perhaps you've spent many years caring for others, you've forgotten how to prioritize yourself. Perhaps you already have clear goals in mind but don't know where to start in achieving them. Maybe it's a simple case of lacking the confidence to go after your dreams. Whatever the reason you hold this book in your hands, if it's guidance to move forward you need, read on.

So, who am I and why should you listen to me? I consider myself an example of how the techniques advocated in these pages can help you to achieve your goals. I've overcome many challenges in my life. I experienced a difficult childhood, I became a single parent and I struggled financially. Through goal-setting, planning and perseverance, I achieved long-held dreams. I wanted to record my experiences, so I wrote a book about them: *#GoalGetter: Strategies for Overcoming Life's Challenges*.

I firmly believe that we, as women, have the power to change, attract and live the life we desire. So, I've created this book with the aim of motivating those of you who've lost the confidence to take action, and inspire you to see the future of your dreams is possible. In this book, you'll find strategies and tactics to help you grow both personally and professionally.

I will be taking you through the seven steps that worked for me: Exploring what it is you really want (step one); understanding why you want it (step two); knowing how to make a start (step three); choosing who you need to have on your team (step four); creating the right environment for success (step five); outlining your critical path to success (step six) and planning your path to success (step seven).

By the time you reach the end of this book, you will have all the tools and insight to make your dream a reality, to ensure you experience growth both personally and in the business of your choice.

While I can provide you with the framework to set you on your path, you are the one who will need to do the work. Be prepared to experience obstacles and hurdles. No road is without its bumps, but you can navigate them to reach your destination. Visualization, combined with a solid plan for achieving each goal, will help you manifest your dream.

A small word of advice before we get started: Change the way you think about setbacks. Frame them more as opportunities for growth. That way, your energetic vibrations will remain high and tuned into success. Also, be sure to celebrate every win, especially the small ones.

You *can* accomplish each and every goal you envisage. So, let's get started, because I want to share with you the seven steps to help you turn your dream to reality and start manifesting the life you desire.

On October 24, 2020, at approximately 12:49pm, I arrived on the island of Jamaica for vacation/workcation. I contemplated cancelling this trip several times. I arrived depleted, overwhelmed, stressed and burned out—mentally, physically and emotionally. During the three-hour flight, in between sleeping, I kept asking, how did I allow myself to get to this point of having absolutely too much to do, and too many responsibilities, most of which were not mine. Don't worry, I will share more with you as we move through the story. I promised myself that the way I left was not the way I would return.

I rarely sleep on a plane journey but it's like I could not keep my eyes open. I missed the snack and beverage run. I missed taking pictures while being in the air. I was knocked out. When I did open my eyes to check my surroundings and the time, that was when my questions resurfaced: How can I change the way I am feeling? How did I allow myself to get to this point? Why has no one around me noticed, or attempted to help me, or say something? Off to sleep again as my eyes became heavier.

We landed and I don't know if it was the difference in air or the reality that I was away from home, family, work, the comforts of everything I knew, during a pandemic, that I felt like I could finally exhale. All this time I had been working at 1000, trying to start and finish work projects, both business and personal. I was trying to be "present" as a wife and mom, and I was attempting to outdo and beat any goals I had set for myself over the last 365 days. Yes, I challenge and compete with myself often, as a push to get things done.

As we moved through the airport, having our temperatures checked and hands sanitized several times along the way, we finally arrived in the lounge area to wait for our driver. I did not check one email or respond to any messages. I ordered a rum punch and sipped it slowly while thinking about what the next few days would hold for me. Once I arrived at the resort, the first thing I did was eat, shower and sleep. I slept pretty much the rest of the day. The balcony was right in front of the ocean. The water was turquoise blue, and trees swayed in the wind. I slid the balcony doors open and stepped out to actually breathe again. It was beautiful. My first response is thank you God for the opportunity to be here when I contemplated not coming several times in a matter of two months. Thank you God for providing me with all that I have, need and want, because it all already existed inside of me. I grabbed the lounge chair and that's where I found my moment and ended the night... on the balcony.

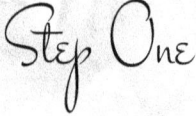

DECIDE WHAT YOU WANT

Think of you and your life as a brand. If you are not happy with what you are currently doing personally and professionally, it's time to change. In fact, not only is it time to change, but you have the power to make the necessary decisions to change. I know it's not as easy as flipping a switch, but we have more tools available than ever before—technology, social media, our own intuition and expanded personal and professional networks.

First, you need to be clear about what it is you actually want out of life. Ask yourself: Where do I see myself in five years? Ten years? A year from now? What is my version of living my best life? And really, what does that mean? Getting caught in the cycle of every day—whatever that looks like for you—is the result of telling yourself that what you have, who you are, and what you do, is satisfying. Meanwhile, you tell your best friend how you wish you could go here and there, do this and that, meet new people, learn new things, and experience an improved quality of life, as if you don't deserve to explore each and every dream, or that anything other than your present is out of reach. Stagnation is the death knell of dreams, because if you can't see anything new, fresh, or different for yourself, you won't exude or attract the energy you need to reach the future you want.

VISUALIZE YOUR FUTURE

Make a list of your wishes. Write down all of them, especially the ideas you feel are just a little too out of reach. You are not limited to the number of dreams you want for yourself, or the areas of your life where they apply. Everything—and I do mean everything: your career, your relationships at every level, your material possessions, your hobbies—is on the table for change. Don't use generic statements like, "I just want to be happy," or "Maybe I'll buy a new car." Be specific. For example, "I want to be promoted to a senior manager role at my firm," or "I want to become an accomplished piano player."

Study your list, and choose one area of your life you want to change. Now envisage the change in your mind. Picture your change happening as if you were already living it. What does it look like? What does it smell like? Who is with you, if anybody? What does it taste like? Where are you? The change you see for yourself must look and feel in your mind and your spirit as natural as breathing.

You must see yourself living the change. Where do you go every day? What are you doing in that place? How do you get there? What does this location look like? Are you in a city, a suburb, or another country? Are you in a house, a condo, in a hut on the beach? What does the interior look like—the color of the walls, style of furniture, flooring, accessories? What are you wearing? What do you eat? Where do you eat? Where do you shop for groceries, clothing, and household items big and small? The more details you provide, the easier it will be for you to really claim the future you see, and to work for it.

VISUALIZATION TECHNIQUES

To help you answer these questions, create a vision board, a collage of words and pictures that display the hopes and dreams associated with the goals you've chosen. This project is all about you; not the dreams you have for your kids or the dreams your parents had for you. Your vision board is dedicated solely to YOU and the dreams you have for yourself. Specifically, this board is about the one major area of your life you want to change. You can create your board digitally, through handy sites like Canva, or purchase a big piece of poster board and dig out a bunch of magazines to cut out photos that represent the change you see for yourself. Don't limit yourself to images. Words have power, especially the ones we say to ourselves. Stand-alone words or phrases that speak to what's most important to you as you begin laying the first stones for the road to your goal. Choose words that convey the life you see for yourself, how you imagine you'll feel once you reach that goal, and that could describe you at the end of your journey.

Now, place your vision board (if you created a physical one) where you'll see it every day. If you used digital tools, make your vision board your screen saver. Having your goals in plain sight is a great reminder of what you're working toward, and serves as inspiration when your energy lags or your spirit feels overwhelmed.

Maybe a vision board isn't really your thing. Instead, can you write down in detail what you see in your mind? Whether you use pen and paper, or your computer, or even your phone, translating the images into words and spilling those words onto paper—physical or digital—helps put your future self into the universe, making it much more likely you'll succeed.

OTHER FORMS OF VISUALIZATION

Visualization helps you achieve your goals, because you're conditioning your brain to feel, hear, see, taste, and smell the success as if it is real. If you can see yourself reaching each and every goal you set for yourself, your subconscious processes your thoughts as reality, and you increase your chance of success. Oprah Winfrey has been quoted as saying, "If you can imagine, you can create," and legendary boxer Muhammed Ali said, "If my mind can conceive it and my heart can believe it, then I can achieve it." I know you're not about to argue with Oprah and The Greatest!

Additional methods you can use to bring your vision to life include prayer, meditation, and daily affirmations. Prayer is a deeply personal conversation between you and God. If you believe, as I do, that God has a path, a purpose, and a promise for us all, you already know you have everything you need inside you to succeed. That's not to say you won't need help from other people on your journey, but opening your heart to Him about this particular hope, this singular dream, will fill you with the confidence you need to make it happen. Feeling God's love is powerful, and taking the time to check in with Him makes all the difference.

Meditation is another tool you can use to truly get in touch with the future you see for yourself. Vishen Lakhiani designed an 18-minute session that addresses six areas of your life to enhance your brain power: love and compassion (connection), gratitude, peace (forgiveness and freedom from negativity), vision, sense of control (intentions for the day), feeling supported (blessing). According to Lakhiani, "It isn't about clearing your mind, it's about engaging your mind and manifesting abundance in every aspect of your life."

Write daily affirmations in present tense, as though you've already reached your goal, but be discerning about what you claim. Your brain can't tell the difference between what's real and what's not, so writing down something like, "I own a business with revenue consistently in the seven figures," or "My book is a best-seller," shifts the way you think and the way you behave. You'll start to embody your affirmations, making the necessary moves to take your declarations from ink on paper to the reality you wake up to everyday. Whatever you put down on paper should relate to the goal you've chosen. It should be specific, but take care to not list too much, so as not to feel overwhelmed.

Now you have your goal in your mind and you can really see yourself living it, how are you going to get there? Use what you see as the end of your journey as the beginning of your plan and work backward to put together your strategy. Whether or not you have a definitive date for your future state honestly doesn't matter. As long as you have the end goal clear in your mind, and you reach a point where you can't think about not making it happen, you can put together the steps for getting there.

A final note: Don't let perfection get in the way of opportunity. I've made plans on top of plans, and plans to get to the plan, and guess what? Nothing ever happened because I was waiting for the perfect moment while I put together the perfect plan. I finally realized I could never put together the perfect anything because I am a flawed human doing her best. I finally realized that my best is good enough. I stopped waiting for perfection and got to work. Perfection is a myth, and you will never achieve it. Start now, so you can intentionally reach your goal.

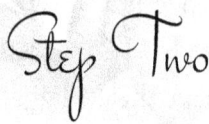

DETERMINE WHY IT'S IMPORTANT TO YOU

Every episode of any police show you watch on TV includes a discussion of motive—why did the perpetrator commit the crime? Answering that question typically leads television detectives to the guilty party. At that point, you nod your head, congratulating yourself on your armchair police work, like, "I knew he was guilty from the minute they questioned him the first time!"

You also have a motive for everything you do in your personal and your professional lives—your WHY. When you get out of bed in the morning, something above anything else propels you through the day. Going to work pays the bills, of course, but there are bigger goals at play here. Let's break them down a bit.

WHY YOU NEED A WHY

The coronavirus pandemic sparked a massive change in the American workplace, the likes of which has never been seen before. Not only did more workers leave their employers in what became known as the Great Resignation, many of those same individuals chose to pursue entrepreneurship. The U.S. Census Bureau recorded 4.4 million new businesses in 2020, the highest total on record, almost 25 percent more than in 2019 and over 51 percent more than the average from 2010 to 2019. What is most striking, though, is WHY so many employees left their jobs and jumped into business ownership. They realized their lives needed to go in another direction in order for them to achieve greater happiness. Or, after working from home with and around their families for months, they were unwilling to return to an office and spend more hours there again than with their loved ones.

Happiness and family are both powerful reasons for making big moves in your life. But they're also pretty general. When you're identifying your why, you need to be specific. We all want to be happy, but what area of your life requires focus and change to produce the happiness you want? Family is also too general. What about your family is pushing you toward change? Dig in and go deep.

WHAT'S YOUR WHY?

Below are some thought starters to help you explore and figure out your why:

- What are your personal values?
- What is your true passion? What did you love to do when you were younger, before other responsibilities took over?
- Why do people come to you? Do you enjoy listening to others, telling stories, giving advice, giving a hug?
- Are you satisfied with your significant relationships? Do you want to improve or end your marriage? Are you and your children close? Do you spend quality time with them? Do they feel safe confiding in you?
- Why do people come to you? Do you enjoy listening to others, telling stories, giving advice, giving a hug?
- Are you satisfied with your significant relationships? Do you want to improve or end your marriage? Are you and your children close? Do you spend quality time with them? Do they feel safe confiding in you?
- What about your parents? Do you have a good connection with them? Do you want a better connection, or should you seek help for hurt you've suffered?
- Are your friendships strong and mutually beneficial? Can you count on your friends when you really need them, and can they count on you?
- Does your career/job give you a sense of purpose? Do you feel you are doing what you were meant to do with your unique gifts and talents? If not, think hard about what your gifts are, what you enjoy, how you can attract more of that into your life through your work.
- Is your life outside home and work fulfilling? Are you

involved with organizations and/or causes that reflect your values? If not, and you had the time and luxury, what causes could you become passionate about?

In short, you need to define your values and examine every corner of your life to determine if the way you live, work, and play is right for you. Take a look at the people in your life—family, friends, co-workers—and ask yourself if they are individuals who share similar world views, ambitions, spiritual beliefs, and more, with you. If there is an area that's lacking, keep asking yourself questions that peel away the layers of how you found yourself in a position to recognize the need for deep change. Most likely, you will find your WHY amongst the answers.

Let me give you an example. A friend of mine, Melissa, was married for almost twenty years, some of it happily. She and her husband, Paul, married young and had three children. Unfortunately, Paul became verbally, emotionally, mentally, and occasionally physically, abusive first to her and their kids. Melissa changed from being a pretty optimistic person who loved openly, to becoming quick to anger, and not leading with love, even when she saw what it was doing to her kids, and passing judgement when she knew better. Melissa knew a few years into her marriage that she and Paul were wrong for each other, but because their oldest child wasn't legally hers, she knew that if she tried to take the kids and leave, Paul would take the child away from their siblings, so she stayed.

For the most part, family life was happy, but the kids avoided Paul whenever he was home. Eventually, the oldest child left for college in the next town. The middle child did almost the same thing. Their youngest child was in their last semester of college when Melissa decided to file for divorce. Her primary reason wasn't to get away from an abusive relationship, though that would have made sense, right? Instead, she'd grown tired of behaving contrary to her true character, and echoing the negative traits she didn't like about Paul in her relationships with each of her children.

A few months later, Melissa attended an event with old friends where women gathered in a circle to visualize their future selves. The visualization exercise went beyond just seeing images in their minds. The organizers had participants draw word clouds that represented where they saw themselves in a day, a month, a year, or several years down the road. Melissa closed her eyes and thoughts surfaced about the way she truly wanted to live: she heard the conversations she wanted to have with her kids; she saw herself hosting a dinner party with close female friends. She felt a sense of purpose, working and playing in a way that put love, compassion, and service at the center of everything she did. After being deeply unhappy for too many years and realizing that life was too short to stay where she knew she didn't belong, Melissa was confident she would leave her marriage once her youngest child graduated from college and was settled into their adult life.

Establishing her new life wasn't always smooth, of course. She needed a job with a higher salary and benefits, she had to find a place to live, and she had to explain her decision to her family. She also had to break the habit of calling Paul every time something happened, whether good, bad, funny, or sad. Melissa felt like half her body was missing for a long time. She did experience improved relationships with her children, which helped her heart heal to a certain extent. What is most important is that Melissa experienced a new level of contentment, of fulfillment, because she had a WHY that could no longer be ignored if she was going to feel anything close to the peace and happiness she'd seen and drawn during the visualization exercise at her friends' event.

Understanding your WHY, and visualizing it in detail, engaging every one of your five senses is all the encouragement you need to make real and lasting change in the area of your life you identified in the previous chapter. However, real change is rarely comfortable, and it can feel so much easier to keep on keeping on. Your WHY will keep you motivated to keep moving, despite setbacks, challenges, and the sheer strength it takes to keep going forward when everything tells you to turn back. Melissa's decision to divorce Paul essentially blew up their family, which she thought she'd prepared for, but the reality of losing Paul's side of the family was a pain she could not have anticipated. She could also not have foreseen how she was the emotional center of her family, and once she stepped away, how her kids would struggle to find their footing. But, like Melissa, your authentic life is waiting for you, and you deserve it. You deserve everything you envision for yourself.

DON'T COUNT *the days*
MAKE THE DAYS *count*

Step Three

HOW TO BEGIN

Now that you've identified your goal, created a vision board, and clearly defined your WHY, you need to commit your plan to paper by jotting down the steps you'll take to make your dream a reality. "Failure to plan is planning to fail," is not just a saying people toss around; it's a fact. So, the list of steps you make isn't metaphorical—it's a map for how you'll make your dream come true. Have you ever heard the saying, "A dream without a plan is just a wish"? This is really no different than the "to do" list you create for tackling household chores, and tasks in the workplace. Without a plan, how can you expect to take your first step, much less finish the journey?

Looking at your goal as though it is a giant mountain to climb can be overwhelming. I know; I've been there. Remember when I said I've made plans for plans, and then a plan for those plans? I was turning around in circles and not getting anywhere. However, learning the SWOT technique changed everything.

THE SWOT ANALYSIS

SWOT is an acronym for strengths, weaknesses, opportunities and threats. It was developed by Albert Humphrey in the 1960s as part of a research project at Stanford University, and it has been used ever since to help both businesses and individuals with their goal planning. Using the SWOT technique enabled me to assess my situation both internally and externally. I learned what I was bringing to the table, as well as what I lacked and what skills I might need to obtain. I also learned that my strengths can lead me to opportunities, and that while I may not have control over possible threats, I can try to plan for and prepare certain courses of action in advance of them occurring.

Below are some thought starters to help to interrogate your own strengths, weaknesses, opportunities and threats.

INTERNAL

Strengths

What do you do well?

What is your gift, talent, or craft?

What resources do you have?

Weaknesses

What areas could you improve in?

What skills are you lacking?

Where do you lack knowledge?

EXTERNAL

Opportunities

Do your strengths open you up to possibilities you hadn't considered before?

Do your weaknesses highlight areas where you can grow into your potential?

What interests can you explore, what trends can you take advantage of?

Threats

What obstacles could prevent you from reaching your goal?

What outside factors might impact your plans?

Can you identify how your weaknesses expose you to threats?

After you've conducted your SWOT analysis for the goal you've chosen, it's time to break the process down into smaller pieces that feel more achievable. Here is an example from my own life where I used the SWOT technique and then the SMART method.

THE SMART METHODOLOGY

I knew my story of overcoming a difficult childhood, single parenthood, financial issues, and more, could help other women find the strength and encouragement to do the same, so I set out to write a book detailing my experiences and approach. That book became *#GoalGetter: Strategies for Overcoming Life's Challenges*. Before I thought about how the book would begin and end, how many chapters I would write, and the topics I would cover, I tackled the question of whether or not I was qualified to write a book like the one I'd imagined. I thought about how I would best use my existing strengths, overcome my inexperience—my weakness, what resources I could take advantage of and what threats might stand in the way of me fulfilling my dream.

It took me years to get out of my own way, but looking back, the process was the same for the first book, second book, and so on.

Strengths: I was a living example of how someone can change their life. I was a good writer who knew how to tell a story. I had the ability to trust my intuition and gut feeling, although starting out it was challenging to do so.

Weaknesses: Prior to my first book, Goal Getter, I had never written a book before, and I didn't know how to get it published.

Opportunities: There were resources available through social media groups and other online portals to help me understand how to self-publish. I had trusted mentors who could guide and encourage me.

Threats: I maintained a busy schedule between family, work, and church, so finding the time to write was going to be challenging. The cost of publishing could also be too high, so I thought.

After reviewing my SWOT analysis, I realized that becoming an author was exactly the right path for me because I was confident I could lay out a path for other women who wanted to change the direction of their lives. I dove in by composing a rough outline to follow, and persisted in moving forward. Of course, as predicted in my threats, life intervened on a number of occasions, and my book was pushed to beyond the back burner. One day, I knew it was time to get serious. My cousin passed away unexpectedly and I started thinking about my own life journey and dreams unfulfilled. So I used the SMART method to set goals and track my progress. SMART is another acronym which stands for specific, measurable, achievable, realistic, and timely. It was originally conceived as a tool for business management to reach goals laid out during annual strategic planning, and individuals use it regularly to assess whether or not they are on track to achieve their goals.

Here is an example, using my own story, of how the SMART method can work:

Goal: I will finish my manuscript in six months.
Specific: I will write one chapter per month.
Measurable: By completing one chapter per month, I will know by the 15th or so of each month if I am on target, and I can adjust my daily word goal accordingly. At the end of the six months, I will have achieved my goal, if I remained consistent.
Achievable: Having considered all the internal and external variables, I am comfortable this goal is within my grasp. I have a computer and a quiet place to work. It is my responsibility to make this happen.
Realistic: I have made an objective analysis of my strengths, weaknesses, opportunities available to me and the possible threats that may hinder my progress, and with all that in mind, I believe this goal is achievable within the timeframe I have set.
Timely: By the end of the sixth month, I will be finished with my manuscript. By completing one chapter per month, I can easily ascertain if I'm staying on task or not.

Notice that I gave myself six months to complete my book, and I broke that bigger goal into smaller pieces that took into account my reality, which also included work, family, church, and more. I needed to pull apart my giant target so I wasn't overwhelmed, and instead felt reassured I could keep the pieces of my life in harmony. Using the SMART method enabled me to keep my motivation high.

I also celebrated the completion of each chapter, and you should do the same every time you cross an item off your list. Rewarding yourself during the course of your journey, and not just at the end of it, is also a great way to keep your energetic vibration operating at a higher frequency so you continue trusting the process when inevitable setbacks occur.

Real change means getting comfortable with discomfort. If you prepare yourself at the beginning for any rough waters you may need to navigate, you'll weather the storms more effectively than you would if you were not prepared for them at all. You are initiating a giant shift in your life, and the upheaval could be more than you thought or it could be less. Either way, you should be ready to take on whatever comes your way that could hinder your progress. That's not to say some things can't be predicted, but overall, you'll feel more confident if you take the time to consider every angle.

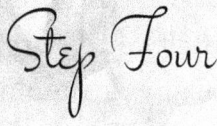

GET YOURSELF A TEAM

How many times have you heard the phrase, "self-made millionaire"? I don't know why people use this description for anyone, really. No one does anything truly on their own because success doesn't occur in a vacuum. Whether you know someone directly, or you know someone who knows someone else, or you find a connection purely by coincidence, you will work with others at some point—most likely at several points—during your journey. And isn't that beautiful? Going it alone and feeling crushed under the weight of not having a circle to lean on is a recipe for burnout and failure.

Here's the thing: You don't have to go it alone!

Speak your plan into existence. When we keep our goal to ourselves, it's far too easy to let it fall by the wayside. We can make up excuses and pass them off as reasons for not completing our tasks, leaving our goals in the dust. How often have you promised yourself you'd start exercising, only to stop going to the gym or walking or running after just a few days? You tell yourself work is too demanding, you're too tired, the kids need you, the holidays are coming, you don't have enough matching athletic outfits to get you through the week. Whatever self-sabotaging reasons you find, you undoubtedly convince yourself your setback is temporary, that you'll resume exercising once life settles down.

But, life is never going to settle down, and it's up to you to put the pieces in place so you can create and stick to an exercise program that works for you. You could go to bed an hour earlier to make it easier to wake up earlier to work out, or you could use your lunch hour to walk or stop at the gym on the way home. In other words, you schedule time for working towards your goals, as you would schedule meetings, parties and kids' extracurricular activities. Its more self-management than time management.

FIND YOUR CHEERLEADERS

If you tell the universe the change you plan to make, and gather the right people to cheer you on, you're more likely to stick with your plan and achieve your goal. If exercising more and improving your health is your goal, you need people to support you, to serve as your workout buddy, and to hold you accountable. The first step, though, is speaking your success—tell the universe what you want and what you are doing to achieve it.

We should also discuss who should have the privilege of knowing you're making a major change in your life. It might be tempting to tell everyone, and why wouldn't you, right? Your growth is good news! In this case, you should be more discerning about who you trust with this information, and limit your circle to those closest to you, and the individuals who will play a role in helping you achieve your goal. I suggest giving folks in your outer circles only vague ideas about what you're planning, but not the details. I know this may sound melodramatic, but undertaking a significant change could make you vulnerable, and you only want the people you are confident will help to know your plans.

Remember my friend, Melissa? She told four people what she was doing and why, and those individuals carried her when she felt like she was falling. They reaffirmed she was doing the right thing for her, and that as a result of taking her power back, she was providing a positive example for her kids, and they provided logistical support like helping her move out of the home she shared with her (now ex-) husband. After she moved, she expanded her circle, but not by much, and she did so because she knew who would question her decision, and who would just ask after what she needed, and provide it.

KEEP YOUR CARDS CLOSE

You need to take the same care whether you're facilitating change in your personal or professional life, or both. We all have people in our lives who are walking definitions of ride or die, and we all have people who ask, "Are you sure this is the best choice?" or "Is that even a business?" If the energy and effort they put into doubting us was instead invested in helping us, well, just imagine how high we could soar!

In many cases, we just need someone to show us the way. I've been fortunate to have four mentors who made a huge difference in my life in so many ways. My first mentor was chosen for me through a program at my high school. Then, as I moved into my young adult and early professional years, I actively sought women in positions I wanted to see myself in after gaining the right experience and appropriate education. I've also had a mentor who simply showed me the ropes of a new position so I would feel more comfortable more quickly. It is always advisable to choose a mentor who is already experienced in the goal you are seeking to achieve.

In addition to speaking your goal into existence, confiding in your circle, and potentially finding a mentor you can emulate, you also need to rely on your networks to help you. "Self-made millionaire" is a myth, don't forget.

USE YOUR CONNECTIONS

Consider the closest to you. Do you know someone who's had a similar experience to you, or who has achieved a goal similar to the one you are hoping to achieve? Perhaps they just passed through this same season of their life and can offer advice in helping you avoid any pitfalls they encountered.

Are you considering advancing your education, but you're unsure about how you'll balance work, family, and school? I'm sure you know someone who's had the same challenge. Actually, I am that person, and it wasn't easy for me to obtain my associate's degree, my bachelor's degree, or my master's degree. I balanced the various aspects of my life as best I could, and sometimes I fell short in one area or another, but you know what? I did it, though I didn't do it alone. I had my own village that rallied around me, and helped me continue to see the light at the end of the tunnel.

If you're looking to change your job or even career, carry out some research into companies you might like to work for. Once you have a few ideas, look through your LinkedIn connections for people you may know who work at your targeted organizations. Reach out to them letting them know you're interested in learning more about any opportunities, and asking if they'd be willing to have a conversation. I bet you nine out of ten people will accept your invitation and potentially direct you to the hiring manager to advance your inquiry, perhaps towards the application process.

If you want to advance a business you own, you may need to consider taking a different approach to the one you've taken up to now. You will need to plan with intention and strategy, and be consistent in your execution. You may need to assess the scalability of your business and really take time to understand what you need in order to expand in a measured and profitable way. You may need to hire someone, or even an entire team, to take your business to the next level. If that's the case, how will you successfully recruit, screen, and interview candidates? If you don't already have an in-house human resources department, you may need the services of a third-party consultant to take care of the heavy lifting required at the beginning of your search. Maybe you've been a solopreneur, and now you're ready to expand the products and/or services you offer, and you need a business coach. Hiring someone to help you reach your goal could be exactly what you need.

When you closed your eyes at the beginning of this exercise and visualized living your dream as if it were your reality, who did you see helping you along the way? Who were the folks you saw yourself leaning on for the support you'll need at every point of your journey? Who did you see celebrating with you when you achieved your goal? Make a list and start there. As you travel your road to success, you will most likely realize you need or don't need additional help, like a coach or an accountant or an assistant.

Success doesn't happen overnight nor does it happen when you try to go it alone. There will be many moments when you'll close your eyes and wonder if it's all worth it. I'm here to tell you that for whatever vision you put together, it is all absolutely worth every minute you use, every penny you spend, and every breath you take to make it come true.

make yourself a priority

CREATE THE RIGHT ENVIRONMENT FOR SUCCESS

Your goal involves a lot of moving pieces, including the physical location(s) of where you'll complete the steps of your journey. If you can complete everything on your journey without a change of scenery, that's great. I have found, though, that spending time outside your normal environment can increase your concentration and productivity. It may even be that your final destination involves a physical relocation. Here are some points to consider:

- Do you need to seek new employment to reach your goal?
- Do you need to move to reach your goal?

- Do you just need time to yourself in a quiet space to achieve your goal?
- Do you need a location separate from your home in which to work on your goals?
- Do you need to hire anyone to help you reach your goal?

FINDING A QUIET LOCATION

When I set out to write my first book, I didn't need anything beyond my computer and a quiet place to work. Luckily, I have an office in my home where I could close the door and concentrate, but it wasn't always like this. Occasionally, I needed to get away from my familiar surroundings, to local coffee shops, the library, the fellowship hall at church, the couch of a friend who worked from home. Simply changing what I looked at when I raised my eyes from my screen was enough to spark my creativity and make me more productive.

Do you ever find that when you're in the shower, or taking a walk, the best ideas come to you? When our brains are allowed to step away from our "executive functions", our minds have more room to be creative. In other words, stepping away from your normal work area provides just enough of a break for our creativity to flow more openly than when we report to the same chair at the same desk every day.

The rush of our daily lives is enough to derail even the most detailed plan, which is why you need a space where you can shut out the sound of kids asking what's for dinner, or your spouse yelling at the game on TV, or where you can take a phone call without interruption. Where you work on your goal is just as important as why you're doing it, when you'll start, who you need to help you, and how you'll pull all the pieces together.

FINDING YOUR OPPORTUNITY AS AN EMPLOYEE

For many of us, training or education gives us the tools to take advantage of opportunities in our careers. Unfortunately, not every employer is structured to facilitate or support our growth, so we need to look elsewhere for opportunities. Perhaps you earned your degree or specialized certification, and your current position no longer fits who you are and who you're working to become. Perhaps you are looking to move somewhere else within the same field, or you've learned new skills and you're ready to spread your wings in a new industry. Perhaps you have your sights set on a corner office, as a member of the C-suite. Or, it may be that a new job is not necessary to support your goal.

You may find your opportunity somewhere different from where you are right now, so the point here is to be broad-minded about what you want and need and where you can find it. Remember your why. Starting a new job with a different company, whether you remain living where you are or you have to move, could be part of the journey because you'll make more money, you'll work with people who can help you, and the position is in a city where you want to live.

EXPLORING ENTREPRENEURSHIP

If you want to start an e-commerce business selling products but not making them yourself, you'll need to identify which vendors you'll use, where they are located and how you'll fulfill orders in a timely fashion. Will you have a warehouse to hold inventory, or will you structure your company as a drop shipper?

If you want to have more control over order fulfillment, shipping, and customer service, storing the goods you sell might be the answer. In that case, you need to secure a building with the right amount of square footage and fill it with the equipment, shelving, offices, and personnel like warehouse associates, managers, IT and development, customer service, and administrative employees.

As a drop shipper (an online retail merchant who sells goods delivered to the consumer directly from the manufacturer), there are still logistics to consider. After connecting with the companies that supply what you sell, you still need a website with enough power and support to sustain an online retail store. You'll still need customer service representatives, marketing, human resources, and more. Where will you find your team? Where will they work?

A brick-and-mortar retail operation requires a location, too. Where do you want your store to be? What will you sell? Where will you get your merchandise? How will it get to your store? How will you recruit your staff? How will you guarantee cash and credit transaction safety? Where will customers park?

HIRING

Most entrepreneurs start their business ownership journey as solopreneurs, which means they do everything on their own—sales, marketing, client work, etc. Recognizing when it's time to hire will help your business grow in revenues and, eventually, profit as well. Where will you find these individuals who can help?

I know several small business owners who belong to valuable groups on social media—Facebook, in particular—where they get support, guidance, and opportunities to network. Some of the groups do require a subscription, but most also have a larger, free group that provides solid value as well. When they began putting a team together or adding to the ones they had, each of these entrepreneurs turned to their groups to find qualified candidates. Don't limit yourself to using your personal and business social media channels. Use your networks. When you operate in your zone of genius, and hand tasks to those who specialize in the areas where you need help, you will decrease your stress and increase your chances of success.

PRODUCTS

Working with individuals who can bolster your strengths can also lead you to products that can make balancing your responsibilities easier to get you over the finish line. Amy is good at math, but she struggles with bookkeeping. Her accountant offers a program for a monthly fee that gives Amy access to software where she can track invoices, payments, and expenses. This software would otherwise be out of reach for Amy. This way she has access to affordable software and she still has a CPA going over her books every month to make sure she stays on track and out of trouble with the IRS.

If you're a retailer with a goal of increasing sales by 20 percent year-over-year, you need a CRM (customer relationship system) to automate a number of steps in your customer journey. You can carry out email marketing, social media management, landing page and sales portal creation and customer satisfaction surveys through a CRM. You will need to do a lot of work up front—loading emails, developing workflows, creating and scheduling social media posts, designing landing pages—but over time, you will see the return on investment in a number of ways. Not only will you have the time to focus on where your talents are best utilized, you'll most likely also experience increased sales and customer satisfaction.

Both of these examples use Saas (software as a service), and because we live in a digital world, most of the solutions you find will most likely involve using a computer or your phone. I still need to keep a planner where I use a pen to schedule my day. I also use two calendars—Google and Outlook—so I know my life remains in sync, no matter which schedule I'm looking at throughout the day. But this is my system. Be sure to create a system that works for you.

SERVICES

As a small business owner who also balances family and a full-time job, I often found myself doing too much on my own. I needed help, and I waited far too long to hire a virtual assistant (VA) to take over the administrative tasks that took so much time away from the activities where my time and talents were most effective.

My V.A. is responsible for creating and scheduling invoices, posting and engaging on social media, managing my calendars, basic data entry, email correspondence, and more. Where my V.A. helps me the most, though, is in conducting research about my industry, like marketplace trends, and handling the bulk of customer service inquiries. Until I hired my V.A, I was doing everything—EVERYTHING—for my business, and I was spread too thinly. I wasn't accomplishing my goals, and I couldn't figure out why until a friend told me about her VA and what a game-changer it had turned out to be. I used freelance services like Upwork and Fiverr to find creators who had the skills I needed at a rate I could afford.

You've pulled together the pieces of your plan and the necessary resources. Now we need to talk about the inevitable trials and tribulations that come with working toward a goal.

Something will go wrong along the way. You will most likely be unable to avoid a pothole or two, so think through every step of your plan and identify where things could go off the rails, and how you'll mitigate any negative fallout to keep moving forward.

Allison has a clothing line she designs herself and has manufactured by a third-party supplier. If she wants to increase the variety of what she offers and how much inventory she stores, Allison has to look at every link in her supply chain for where it could fall apart and potentially delay production and delivery. What if the particular brand of t-shirt Allison uses is unavailable? Does she have a backup of similar quality? What if the manufacturer can't meet her deadlines? Does Allison have another vendor she can work with to fill orders? What if shipping delays across the industry impact her promised delivery dates? Has Allison developed a line of communication with her customers to alert them to delays, and an offer to compensate them for their inconvenience?

Remember Melissa who divorced her husband? She had to imagine possible scenarios that would have interrupted her plan, and come up with a corresponding solution. What if Paul's car didn't start the day she was moving out, and he didn't go to work? Melissa was determined to make her vision a reality, and she talked to the moving company to ensure a team was available the next day. What if the movers canceled at the last minute or just didn't show up? She had another moving company scheduled and reserved on her credit card (without being charged so Paul wouldn't see it) for two hours after her original appointment. What if one of their kids came home unexpectedly? Melissa knew this possibility was the most difficult to work through, but she also knew honesty would be the best policy, and she was prepared to have that conversation if necessary. What if Melissa couldn't find a job in the city where she wanted to live? She had never been afraid of hard work, and she knew she might have to work two jobs for a period of time until she landed a new position with the right salary and benefits.

By imagining what could go wrong, and expecting that what may go wrong might go wrong, you'll be better prepared to make the necessary adjustments to keep you moving forward. This is not to say you will be able to preplan, predict and solve all the problems, but thinking through scenarios will make you more aware of possibilities, or a lack thereof.

Now let's talk about the party! How will you celebrate crossing those items off your to-do list as your start realizing your vision? Yes, you absolutely must celebrate in whatever fashion feels the most appropriate. Was your goal to buy your first or a new home? Have a house-warming! Was your goal to move into that corner office? Treat yourself to dinner and that pair of shoes you've been eyeing! Was your goal to start your business? Raise a glass to yourself! Was your goal to leave your 9-to-5 because you wanted your side hustle to be your only hustle? Have a night out with friends who can toast to your success!

When you reach your goal, you will have accomplished a major milestone. You. Did. It! Be proud! Be happy! And yes, hell yes, celebrate and bask a little in the light of a job well done. You deserve it!

GET RID OF SELF-LIMITING BELIEFS

Here I am four and a half years in business. History says that most businesses fail within the first five years, so there I was thinking I was making progress with therapy, self-limiting beliefs, and this pandemic happens. Instinctively, the old me was thinking, I knew it was too good to be true. I am right on target with failing, says the statistics. What we feed our minds matters. I knew I had to do something quickly to cast down those thoughts, so whenever they surfaced, I had to provide a comeback for them.

Failing in the first five years of business didn't have to be my story simply because it was the norm. But, how could I look around me and be inspired when everything was predicting doom and gloom? And that was my mission. I had to shift too, and trust me it came with some dragging of my feet and questioning if what I was doing would work. No ifs, ands or butts, I had to make certain decisions. I had to shift how I was doing business. I had to shift plans that I had in place. I had to shift my way of thinking and I had to be resourceful. I had to pivot not knowing what to expect, only to trust the process and know my decision was necessary.

I had been planning my very first LIVE event. I had the venue under contract, I'd started marketing the event and was feeling really confident in how things were going. As the event neared, new social distancing guidelines were released and this threw a wrench in my plans. There I was, as a new business owner, offering refunds, so my integrity and reputation were intact while still moving forward with other work obligations. This really was a pull on my emotions. I was emotionally drained. However, I've always been results driven. I couldn't sit around and wallow in pity and sadness. I had to figure out my next move.

One person that helped me understand some of this, and I don't think she even knows it, was my business coach. I remember hearing her saying something like 'if someone paid you for a ticket, you should be able to refund the money', which meant, you shouldn't be broke. Because of what she initially shared, I had compartmentalized my event. Ticket revenue, marketing, food and beverage and additional expenses that I knew I would incur. I didn't have all the figures in ink but I knew not to touch that ticket money. Another key thing she shared was 'don't try to do everything at once'. Pick one thing and do that one thing.

WHAT DID COVID AND MY COACH TEACH ME?

I developed a greater business sense. I learned from my mistakes. I was learning to separate my emotions from the business and I wasn't sweating the small stuff. This kept me focused. This further peaked my level of creativity, and I became more driven in terms of how I could serve my community and clients. I was now grown, although a baby in business, but in a short time, I was learning valuable lessons about life and simultaneously about business. I was investing in myself and viewing money as an exchange of energy. As long as I had my heart and hands open, I would receive, but as long as I kept my heart and hands closed, nothing could enter. What did this do for me personally? I was still on the path of self-exploration to rid myself of those self-limiting beliefs. I wanted to learn more and more about myself because somehow, along the way from childhood to adulthood, my vision became distorted.

ASSESS YOUR CURRENT STATE OF BEING

In order to manifest something (in my opinion) you first have to assess where you are and also decide what you want to be, do or have. Let me give you a glimpse of how it showed up in my personal life.

I honestly did not think it would be possible for me to ever get married again. I felt like I was scarred. I remember describing myself to my now husband as "damaged goods". Who would want me? There I was telling my future husband and past boyfriend (long story) about how I was not worthy of being in a relationship with anyone and that included him. As a matter of fact, and I am sure he can confirm this and even finish my sentence, my words to him were specific: "I'm not looking for a relationship and I will call you if I need you (wink, wink)". He chuckled but I was dead serious. I did not want to invest the time, energy and resources into another member of the male species. I had lost time to make up and the first item on the agenda was ME. What I did not know at the time was that I sounded crazy as hell, saying 'I'm not ready for a relationship', or 'I am not worthy of a relationship so let me "settle" for what I can get when I can get it'. I thought I was practicing control and calling the shots, but looking back I was belittling myself. How thoughtless can I be? There I went dating someone who I thought was already emotionally unavailable, as he had his own share of trauma to deal with and baggage to unpack. When we reflect on how we started we both giggle at the conversation. Two imperfect and flawed individuals with baggage to unpack.

Now let me back up to the in between relationship period. I was trying to read every self-help book there was, crying out to God asking for help— emotionally and mentally. I was practicing self-control because I thought I was calling the shots. I was in control of me, yet I was referring to myself as "damaged goods". Where did that term come from, and why would I refer to myself that way. Damaged because something didn't work out? Damaged because someone couldn't acknowledge the treasure they'd found? Damaged because I was not where I thought I should be? Damaged goods was the only way to describe how I felt.

I would confide in my uncle about a lot of things. He was who I had looked up to; he was a father figure to most of his nieces and nephews (sleep in peace). My mother's baby brother was left to be the "go to person" of the family. Everyone knew and loved Uncle Nate. He used to always say to me, "Niecey, things get greater later". In my head, it was like a broken record—something I had heard before and wasn't ready to accept because I was tired of waiting, and it wasn't even a long time. Why can't my greater later be now? This taught me patience.

Yes I was the type that wanted quick fixes and microwaveable results immediately This was my same approach with relationships, including marriage. Now, realizing that everything is a process and timing is a part of it, I had to learn what I am always telling my clients to do now... TRUST THE PROCESS! There was a lot that I had to learn about me. This is where the self-love came in. I wanted to get to the root of why I was feeling that way. Instead of considering the "stigma" that only people who are crazy go to therapy, I sought help for myself. I felt in my heart that if I got myself together then it would flow outward. The root of the tree was my heart and if my heart was right, it would grow branches, and those branches would be extended to everything around me: family, business, community and so on. I had to learn how to have a high regard for my own wellbeing. I had to learn how to take care of my own needs first. I had to learn how to expect more, because settling was something I had become accustomed to.

Self-love meant checking my belief systems and being conscious enough to acknowledge them without the critical eye but reinforce new words in my vocabulary, and new thoughts in my mind. I had to really assess my self-limiting beliefs and deal with the fear and doubt that always showed up as twins to talk me out of doing whatever I had initially set my mind to do. So, you know what I started doing? I started exploring. Exploring beyond the self-limiting beliefs. The self-limiting beliefs kept me in hiding, playing safe, in fear. I was limiting the belief that I could ever possibly love again and be loved, so what did I do? I exhibited the behavior to line up with what I thought.

How did this play out? It played out in my thoughts, my actions and my words (damaged goods). I am almost cringing and shaking my head now thinking about that term. Don't think that's the only bad word I said to myself. It wasn't. I was extremely critical of myself, in general. I never felt like I was doing enough. Because I was in the place of discovering, exploring, wanting better and feeling (not knowing) that this couldn't be it, I was still searching for something, although I didn't know what that something was. My microwaveable results didn't happen. The overnight love story didn't exist, but the way I love myself is so different compared to before. Just like I had imagined, if I get myself right then other things will fall into place. Thankfully, some things fell into place while I was in the process of exploring and discovering myself. I love how I have evolved as a wife, mom, sister and daughter. I love how I have changed as a woman. I love how I am able to show up as my most authentic self. I love the grace that I extend to myself. Most importantly, I love the peace that came with it.

Now let me share how it showed up in my business life. On November 17, 2020, I woke up thinking about my business and the people I desire to serve. Automatically, the thought popped up in my head, 'what if I run out of people to serve? What happens to the business?' Do you see how absurd that is? I actually had that thought in mind. Of the billions and billions of people in this world and my thought was there may not enough people to serve.

The truth of the matter is, that was what I had thought, but I know I am not alone. Thoughts like this exist and lead to comparisons with others, paralysis analysis, overthinking, feeling stuck and lacking creativity. While I am grateful to quickly pivot from those thoughts, I still had to deal with why did those thoughts even came up. There I was frantically trying to build a life I felt I deserved, with a lifestyle that I don't need a vacation from, and my survival instincts were about to kick in.

That's what I know... survival. I am a 'make it happen' kind of woman so as much as I desire to live in the present and right now, but plans and thoughts drift into the future. For me, it was about survival yet again. What if? How will I? The choice was mine. I could either travel down that rabbit hole thinking about the what ifs, or I could deal with reality and shift my thinking. I know from past behavior, overthinking caused me to not move. When I am not moving, I start feeling stuck and lack creativity because I am so focused on what is going on within and immediately around me. This leads to paralysis analysis.

SELF-IDENTIFICATION

So how do I start thinking differently? Identify the behavior, acknowledge what it is and make a decision in how I move with my thoughts, words and actions. I know that I am capable of learning. I know that I have gifts. I know that I have purpose (we all do). I know that I am a survivor, a planner and a brilliant being. I may not feel this way all the time but I know this to be true because of past experiences. I had to draw on what I knew to be true. Somewhere along the way, I learned or thought that to give myself credit was boastful. I learned or thought that to point out my strengths was bragging. I learned or thought that to have a high regard or esteem for myself was conceited. This is the furthest from the truth.

Here's what I do know and have learned: Success, purpose, love, gratitude and so many other words are defined by the individual and not by others. My idea of success may not be someone else's idea of success. My idea of what love is or not is "my" idea. My gratitude is not someone else's. Therefore, survival is different for everyone. Survival means that you overcome something. I am sure we all have done that—mentally, physically, emotionally, financially or spiritually. So, that would make us all survivors, right? I had to retrain my thoughts.

This leads me to of course talk about my faith in God. God wants me to have the desires of my heart. Everything I need is already inside of me and whatever is not in me is in someone else. If I can't do it then I can hire someone else who can. At the end of the day, the goal and mission is to bring what I have to life and to attract and live the life I desire. It's been tough moving the needle from survival mindset to abundance mindset, but the shift is happening. Survivial is what I know and abundance is my God given birthright. Survival lets me know that come hell or high water, I am a 'make it' kind of woman. Abundance lets me know that God has got me, and the good and bad is still working out for my good. Words are so powerful! It took me to pause, assess and process my journey thus far for me to be able to speak in this manner.

I am fearfully and wonderfully made
I am a billionaire in the making
I am a queen
I am a woman of integrity
I am gratitude
I am love
I am peace
I am...

If you haven't been doing so, NOW is the time to start affirming yourself. It's not bragging, being conceited and looking down on others, as some of us might have been trained or taught. It is realizing that you are who you are and you are a gift to this world. Isn't it amazing that out of all the people in this world, God saw fit to bring you into it. God saw fit for our paths to cross. God saw fit for you to have the desire to read my book about manifestation and success. God saw fit to give you a message. God saw fit to keep you. There's more I can say but my request for you is to affirm who you are, even if it's a few words. Get in the habit of doing this daily. This is what helped me and I pray it helps you too.

Finish these...
I AM _____
I AM _____

I AM _____
I AM _____
I AM _____

It doesn't say I WAS. We are affirming the present! We are setting the expectation.

What has worked for me is having tunnel vision. Only seeing, dealing with and moving toward that thing I desire. Getting rid of the "extra" stuff that doesn't support my mission or cause.

TAKE ACTION

One way for something to manifest and for you to move toward success is to take action. Do something! I remember the thought of writing a book popping into my head well over 25 years ago. I remember the thought of starting a business well over 20 years ago. I had the desire but didn't have the confidence. I had the idea but I didn't initially have the plan. So, what happened with the desire and the idea? Absolutely nothing! I didn't act on it and I wasn't doing anything mentally or physically to ensure it became a reality. Basically, I was wishing but I wasn't intentionally working toward it.

When I set the intention, created a plan and worked diligently and consistently toward it was when I saw it actualize before my eyes. That's with anything. If I had the desire to go back to college and graduate after dropping out as a freshman then I had to make sure my actions, words and deeds were aligned. So what did that mean for me? That meant that I had to complete paperwork, assess my finances, which ended up being student loans because I couldn't afford it, meeting with college faculty, registering for classes, actually going to class, studying, getting help when needed, staying the duration, pushing through obstacles, managing my time, missing some celebrations, sacrificing other things along the way, but resulting in a college degree. It took work. It took consistency. It took diligence. It took action.

I wasn't just sitting waiting for it to happen. I had to figure it out, make it happen and be okay with making some mistakes along the way. This brings me to the thought of making mistakes. It happens. I was always so hard on myself. I didn't want to make a mistake and I didn't want to fail. We put an enormous amount of pressure on ourselves wanting everything to be perfect, no bumps, no dips and no turns. The truth is, some things we don't have control over and have to learn to go with the flow. Mistakes can be costly but mistakes are a way to foster learning. From mistakes, we learn how to do things differently or what went wrong if we take the time to assess the situation. Mistakes, in my opinion, stretch us. When a mistake is made it might cause us to examine ourselves or examine the situation. With this new learned information from the mistake, we can either try again or we can decide to go another route. Either way, we are more informed.

But let me share with you what happens when a mistake was made. Before, I would beat myself up, figuratively speaking. I would internalize everything, wondering and thinking how I could have avoided it or what I could have done differently. It's not a bad thing to assess and learn, I think it's more disheartening when we make mistakes and don't learn from the mistakes, or we blame everything and everyone for the mistake instead of reflecting on our own accountability. When we don't learn, we minimize our chances of growing. I'm sure you are interested in learning AND growing, just like me.

But let's refocus back to self-limiting beliefs. Beliefs have a purpose, self-limiting or not. We have to determine the validity of the belief. Be okay with questioning them, testing them, tossing them if they are not serving a "good" purpose for you, and creating new beliefs. Sometimes, it will require you to replace the old with the new just like we've had to unlearn and get rid of bad habits. It takes time but the first step is knowing and acknowledging where you are.

It Always Seems Impossible Until It's Done

Step Seven

PLAN YOUR PATH TO SUCCESS

Planning your journey absolutely must include benchmarks and a deadline. If you don't build a timeline for when you'll complete each task in order to reach your goal, you won't hold yourself accountable, and your dream may never come true. Remember the SMART goals we talked about during Step Three? "M" is for measurable and "T" stands for timely, otherwise known as benchmarks and a deadline.

This is where you set a target completion date and work backwards to reverse engineer the process to get you there. My best advice is to start as soon as possible and to use a paper calendar that sits on your desk—or one you can carry with you for frequent reference (pocket calendar or your phone). Make sure you list not just your deadlines for each step of the process but also when you plan to do the associated activities. Think of these tasks as you do your "to do" list for work, or the grocery list you make every week, and block the applicable time on your schedule to get them done.

If your dream is to travel abroad for the first time, you have a number of decisions to make:

- Where will you go?
- When will you travel? Your location(s) will help you decide what time of year to book your trip.
- How much will your trip cost? You might have to save for a few months before departure.

These are basic questions that will lead you to form a detailed plan, so you can arrive at the airport relatively stress-free, with luggage and necessary documents in hand. Donna is a single woman who always wanted to visit Spain, and she knew that to get the experience she dreamed about, she was going to have to carefully budget for six months after she put down a non-refundable deposit. Additionally, Donna planned to use a tour company to visit various cities and then walk as much as possible to various historically significant sites, restaurants, and shopping areas. After consulting with the tour company about the best time of year to explore Spain, Donna booked her trip in the fall for the following May and started preparing. She calculated how much she would need to save every pay period, started visiting the gym an extra day per week to build up her stamina, and researched top restaurants in the country's most famous cities. Donna put together a SMART goal with frequent touch points to monitor her progress.

GO INTO THE DETAILS

Some parts of your goal may require you to put in place a multi-step process to complete them, and if you're relying on the contributions of others to close the circle on those pieces, you'll need to take into account how much time each person will need to finish their work. For example, if you hire a career coach to help move you into the executive ranks at your employer, they may need to conduct research on the company, looking at current executives and the occupants of the C-suites. They'll also need to have several conversations with you to determine how to focus on your history, during your current and previous employment, and how you will contribute to the achievement of the business's objectives. While you have your ambition set on growing your skillsets and experience, the bottom line is that promoting you into a role of greater leadership has to benefit the organization. A career coach can advise you on a well-rounded approach to achieving your goals by conducting a SWOT analysis with you, and that takes time you need to build into your SMART goal.

BUILD IN CONTINGENCIES

Moving up the corporate ladder takes perseverance, and you may need a Plan B if an opportunity at your current firm isn't available. How much time will you allow to achieve your goal at your current employer? When will you begin searching for a new position, if need be? Will you use a transition coach to help you identify openings and prepare materials for application when opportunities arise? When will you hire that person, and how much time will you give them to show results?

Let's say you've been thinking about starting a side hustle that you'll eventually want to transition into, or you're ready to make the leap into full-time entrepreneurship. What is your target date for that transition? Now, work backwards to develop your timeline:

- Deadline: When will you launch your business?
- Do you need to find space outside your home?
- How much of an emergency fund do you need to save?
- How far in advance of your launch do you need to have a site secured?
- When will you begin marketing your product and/or service?
- How often will you participate in marketing activities to boost your profile and sell your product and/or service?
- When will those campaigns take place?
- Do you need to hire staff? When will you start that process, and for how many positions?

For years, I've contemplated pursuing my PhD, and I've been actively working through both a SWOT analysis and composing my SMART goal. I, currently, have a full life: work, marriage, family, business, the CEO Wife brand, writing this book, helping women become authors by creating anthologies, and other commitments. I am not 100% all in right now and I need to carefully examine this season of my life as well as and how long I'll give myself to earn my degree. I'll need help from my husband and my children to keep me on track and take care of any number of items normally on my "to do" list. I will require a detailed schedule that brings the pieces of my life into greater harmony to help me achieve this goal should I decide to pursue it.

Most of our lives are scheduled—work hours, family activities, fun with friends, going to the movies, binging your favorite show on Netflix, and more. We wouldn't have the structure we need in order to attend to any of it without blocking time. Establishing a timeline for making your dream come true, to reaching your goal, is critical to your success.

Afterword

> *"Success is where preparation and opportunity meet."* —Bobby Unser, American car racer

And, finally...

I'm going to congratulate you now, even if you haven't started on your journey. That you want to set a goal and develop a plan to reach it, is worthy of recognition. Your success will be predicated on the combination of your will, your plan, and preparing for and finding resolutions for setbacks when they occur. You should be proud of yourself!

Our biggest obstacle is often the excuses we tell ourselves about why we shouldn't do something. But, you've chosen to quiet that voice and focus instead on pursuing the vision and dream life you want and deserve. You've chosen to seek help to manifest your goal into reality by first reading this book so you have an instruction manual on how to make it happen.

When I saw myself as an entrepreneur, I didn't have a detailed guide to help me start, which is why I wrote this book. So much of what I've discussed in these pages is help I wish I'd had at my fingertips when I launched my business. I learned through hiring a coach, investing money in my personal and business development, as well as trial and error, and you will too. However, knowing your WHY and having a plan that brings your goal to life will make all the difference.

Don't forget to celebrate along the way, because you deserve it. I had to remind myself of that too. Now, get out there and be great. I can't wait to see what you do!

References

https://www.salesforce.com/blog/small-business-pandemic-entrepreneurs/

https://eig.org/news/the-startup-surge-business-formation-trends-in-2020

https://www.census.gov/econ/bfs/index.html

#dreamyourplan

Vision Plan

What do you envision for your life?

_____

_____

_____

_____

_____

What are your current challenges?

_____

_____

_____

_____

_____

How can you overcome them?

_____

_____

_____

_____

_____

_____

SMART goals

Create your own SMART goals that align with your vision and plan. Revisit Step 3 if you need to.

SPECIFIC

MEASURABLE

ATTAINABLE

REALISTIC

TIMELY

Support Team

Who do you need to support you and what kind of support do you need? Record names, contact details and notes of your contact.

Virtual Assistant

Mentor / Coach

Spouse / Partner

Trusted friend / Other

Children

Celebrate milestones

What are your weekly, monthly and quarterly milestones?
How will you celebrate them?

WEEKLY
_____

MONTHLY   QUARTERLY
_____   _____

Celebrate milestones

What are your weekly, monthly and quarterly milestones?
How will you celebrate them?

WEEKLY

MONTHLY

QUARTERLY

Celebrate milestones

What are your weekly, monthly and quarterly milestones?
How will you celebrate them?

WEEKLY

MONTHLY

QUARTERLY

Affirmations

I am a billionaire in the making

I am a queen

I am a woman of integrity

I am gratitude

I am love

I am peace

Now write your own...

_____

_____

_____

_____

_____

_____

_____

_____

_____

_____

_____

_____

_____

Task checker

Write down tasks to be completed within the next 30-45 days.

- [ ]
- [ ]
- [ ]
- [ ]
- [ ]
- [ ]
- [ ]
- [ ]
- [ ]
- [ ]
- [ ]
- [ ]
- [ ]
- [ ]
- [ ]
- [ ]
- [ ]
- [ ]
- [ ]
- [ ]

Task checker

Write down tasks to be completed within the next 30-45 days.

- [ ]
- [ ]
- [ ]
- [ ]
- [ ]
- [ ]
- [ ]
- [ ]
- [ ]
- [ ]
- [ ]
- [ ]
- [ ]
- [ ]
- [ ]
- [ ]
- [ ]
- [ ]
- [ ]
- [ ]

Task checker

Write down tasks to be completed within the next 30-45 days.

- [ ]
- [ ]
- [ ]
- [ ]
- [ ]
- [ ]
- [ ]
- [ ]
- [ ]
- [ ]
- [ ]
- [ ]
- [ ]
- [ ]
- [ ]
- [ ]
- [ ]
- [ ]
- [ ]
- [ ]

Acknowledgments

Thank you God for life, health, strength and guidance.

Thank you to my husband, daughters, and circle of sisters for accepting me just as I am. Your love and support mean the world to me.

About the Author

Tamara Mitchell-Davis is a 7x bestselling and award-winning author, wife, mother, and CEO of TM Davis Enterprises, LLC. She holds an MBA and an 085 School Business Administrator Certification from the State of Connecticut and serves as an adjunct faculty member in the Business Department at Asnuntuck Community College in Connecticut. Her published works include *#GoalGetter: Strategies for Overcoming Life's Challenges, Goodbye Fear, Hello Destiny, Blessed Not Broken (Vols.1, 2, 3 and 4)* and coauthor in *Dear Momma*, all available on Amazon and at Barnes and Noble and other retail outlets.

Awards include: 100 Women of Color (Class of 2017) for leadership and community service; ACHI Magazine Orator of the Year (2019); Women of Elevation Triumphant Author (2019); I Am H.E.R International Woman on the Rise and CEO of the Year (2021).

Media appearances include *Women of Distinction Magazine, SwagHer Magazine, Voyage Dallas Magazine, Voyage ATL Magazine, Black Women Mean Business Magazine, Inquiring News,* and *Making Headline News.*

She is an active member of Delta Sigma Theta Sorority, Incorporated. You can connect with Tamara at info@theceowife.com, or visit her website at www.theceowife.com.

Tamara resides in Connecticut with her husband and their children.

facebook.com/theceowife

instagram.com/theceowife860

www.ingramcontent.com/pod-product-compliance
Lightning Source LLC
Chambersburg PA
CBHW070316120526
44590CB00017B/2697